POPULAR MUSIC

Popular Music
by Kelly Schirmann

Black Ocean
Boston · Detroit · Chicago

Black Ocean
P.O. Box 52030
Boston, MA 02205
blackocean.org

Cover Art and Design by Jason Fiske | jasonfiske.cc
Book Design by Janaka Stucky | janakastucky.com

ISBN 978-1-939568-15-1

Names: Schirmann, Kelly.
Title: Popular music / Kelly Schirmann.
Description: Boston : Black Ocean, [2016]
Identifiers: LCCN 2016009071 | ISBN 9781939568151 (alk. paper)
Classification: LCC PS3619.C394 A6 2016 | DDC 811/.6-dc23
LC record available at http://lccn.loc.gov/2016009071

FIRST EDITION

Hey Jay

The infiltration of art by meaninglessness
threatens the ability of art to be taken seriously
Anyway
It's a beautiful song
I don't know what else
you want me to say

I

I have several theories as to what, exactly, music is.

One of them starts in the same place I started, walking the wet beaches of Northern California in silence, feeling an unused language well up inside me and then disappear, over and over again. I built big, beautiful structures in my mind, and when they outgrew me I set them in motion. I watched them go away from me then, quiet and purposeless, into the morning fog.

Another one has to do with trucks, and how my body was stretched out in the back of one once, coming down the long logging road back home in the dark, looking up to where the stars touched the woods. How the girls up front were bickering in Spanish, and how when they finally picked up a local station, the first heavy notes of "Smells Like Teen Spirit" cutting through the static, how they all stopped and went *OHHH* in unison, singing along in broken English all the way down the hill, the wind moving in the tops of the trees.

Another one is the wind in general, the way it doesn't really stop and start so much as it just moves along with you for a little while, attaching itself to your clothing and belief systems, changing your hair and your skin temperature in the same way that it changes everyone's hair and skin temperature (in very different ways).

I know music is an art form. I know this because music, like poetry or painting, is a means of creative expression that is aesthetically pleasing and also completely unnecessary. This is not to say, of course, that art does not have a *place*. It simply means that art does not have a *job*. It makes sense then, at least to me, that it should spend its days doing whatever the hell it wants.

This is also not to say that music is not useful, though I'm not sure it's utilitarian. We may *need* these things to exist in the world, but we don't need them in a literal sense, the way we need food or water or oxygen. And though I do deeply *desire* art's existence, this is arguably just because I desire to live in a *world* that desires art's existence. It pleases and relieves me when I see the World choosing it, because it means that the World is still capable of prioritizing beauty over utility, and that by proxy, so am I.

Music, like Art, is an abstraction. The word itself, leaving my mouth, feels both generally positive and completely formless, even in sound, like a handful of water. I can never be certain when I say the word *music* whether the person I am speaking to is thinking of birdsong, or Beethoven, or a more conceptual *music*—harmoniousness, resonance, order. I am urged by the World (myself) to believe that all three are Spiritual, although whether this applies to their action or their ritual or their product is unclear.

Music is all three of those things; probably countless other things as well. In this way, I find music to be just like everything else in the world—formless, endless, basically nameless, and still: subject to the same construction and categorization as everything else that threatens to transcend our own understanding of it.

6

I'm not sure particles have anything to do with it, really. No words like Wave or Frequency. No *facts* at all. Before we understood sound to be vibrating constantly, like our own small bodies, it was a whole object. It could come from within you, or lay itself on top of you, or move beyond you entirely, on down the road from wherever it came.

I am familiar with many roads in America, but not all. Most of these roads I wouldn't even recognize by sight, or begin to guess what the air smells like there, let alone who it is that lives way down at the end of it. All I can do is listen and think.

Once I heard a story about aboriginal tribes in Australia using songs to map locations to the major landmarks of their territory—Water, Large Rock, Animal Herd. The songs were encoded so that only tribal members would be able to decipher the instructions; outsiders that attempted to follow the directions within the songs would be misdirected, led away from the boundaries of the singing tribe's land, from their water or rocks or meat. In this way, the song was preserved as an honorable gift, and the members of opposing tribes preserved as honorable beings.

I don't know if music is honorable, but I do think it is a gift. Not a charitable or self-righteous gift, but more like it's something you can do for yourself, unceremoniously, instead of lying down in your own bed alone, with the mind's wind scattering its leaves.

Some cultures use music as a way to channel or communicate with the divine. The breath (spirit) and the body (material) are offered in tandem through the physical practice of incantation, which exhausts the body and empties the mind. Into this new clean void, God may enter. I don't know what happens to music after that.

At this point in civilization, it's easy to understand where music comes *from*, which is simply *everywhere*. Each day, moving my body into various buildings and institutions, I am bombarded with powerful messages. Often, I won't realize that anyone has given me any information at all. Then suddenly, activated by some combination of light or memory, they begin to fall out of my own mouth, often for days at a time. What exactly they are doing in my body, between the time they come in and the time they go out, is unclear.

What I do know is that music is powerful, and that it produces its own kind of energy, which we constantly demand. We ask it to fill the majority of the spaces we occupy—living rooms, banks, bars, restaurants, department stores. Increasingly, we even ask it to occupy the spaces we move *through*—a commute, a holiday, an exercise routine, a period of intense depression.

And it does move us, or else it carries us, or else we carry it. Whatever happens, music goes and so do we. It coaxes us onward in the direction of our choosing, providing only an enhancement of a feeling we've already committed to, like salt. And somewhere in this seamless companionship is where I really begin to get lost.

Because it seems, potentially, that *I* am music, that I am made of it, or that it is stored in me, or that it needs to pass through my body to become what it is, or that I don't entirely exist unless I shape my body alongside it.

I hear holiday music in the doctor's office, and suddenly I am aware that it is the Holiday Season. Or did I, deep down, fully conscious of the month and weather, somehow have a hand in creating the messages beaming down on me, which also reflect my mood about them, and which are also solely committed to telling me what I already know?

I don't know if there is anything to gain, or if there has ever been anything to gain, from attempting to describe the indescribable. I don't know if, hacking away at the Thing with our language axe, we actually get closer to defining its shape. In trying to pin it down, we lose the truth of it almost at once—lost as it gets in its own abstraction, lost as we get in the history of others who have attempted to do the same.

What I do know is that music is helpful. It is a means of locating the Thing, by which I mean the Truth, or at least of moving me closer and closer.

When I listen to it, I am listening to the sound of someone discovering something, the sound of being momentarily held in a rhythm to which I can only ever be a witness. If I sing along, I am approximating the act of this discovery in my own body: in solidarity, in preparation. If I listen closely, if I even care to, I can see the outline of what they are looking at. I can walk down the road with them a bit, and ask them how they found it, or what they think it means. Sometimes they tell me; very often they don't.

I know music is talking to me, simply because I am always listening to what it says. When I stop listening, it stops speaking. It becomes music again, and translucent. Whether it ceases to exist altogether, or whether it just ceases to exist to me, is both fascinating and pointless to consider, like almost every other idea on earth. Like a feeling, music has the ability to dominate me entirely, and then vanish at once. And, like a feeling, it enters and exits only when I ask it to.

So I ask it to. When I want to wallow, I get music to dig a hole in the earth. I lay down inside of it, repeating what it tells me: endless and beautiful ruminations, a well-organized grid of suffering. Somewhere deep in my body, the incantation plants itself and begins to vibrate. I can stay there like that, moving and not moving, for several weeks.

When I want to celebrate, I let music build the mountain of itself before me. I allow myself to envision the view from the top: a cloudless arena, the streak of my body moving across it. I hear the joyous cries from the peaks and I follow them upward, my footsteps in line with the rhythm of something that promises only to increase itself. I go onward then, with this new heartbeat, watching each part of the world unfurl itself like a flag below.

Music gives us permission, even encouragement, to experience our own feelings. It accentuates our elation or despair, which is to say it normalizes our elation or despair. It leads us into them, invites us to disintegrate entirely within them, and then asks us to wander in deeper still, trusting only in the voice that leads us, singing.

Singing.

How you could be a person, and therefore imperfect, and still bring an idea into your body so carefully and entirely that when you repeat it back out into the world, it *rings*. How there is a kind of charm and beauty in it, even when it's done badly. How, in fact, we crowd ourselves into dingy bars and cramped booths *just* to sing badly to one another. How this endears us to each other further still.

Singing has nothing to do with music, but it's also the only reason why music is made. Or maybe it's the only way to tell that music actually *works*: little paper lanterns on the river of our collective mouth.

I don't know what the singing is saying, or whether I am even listening. I feel what they mean, I think, as in I think I hear it, somehow. Are they in there? Am I?

Words are so slippery, and still, they are what we have. We give them to one another every day—little dried leaves of them, clouds of them, gleaming commercial banners of them, thousands of scraps of scratched-on papers. I don't know if we direct them, receive them, or simply maintain them. I hope we know we can create them. I hope we can believe in what we create.

When I sing, I am not always singing my songs. I sing men's songs, children's songs, songs of anger and grief, wordless songs, travel and work songs, songs about love that doesn't belong to me, that I could never understand, songs that command or question or hide. The *I* is not me, the words are not mine, and yet: it is, and they are.

Music gives me permission and encouragement to experience the feelings I have *never* had, that maybe I never will. The words themselves do not need to be mine, or even true, for me to understand them, to learn from them. I can memorize them, repeat them, and carry them with me for as long as I need to. They are practice. Whenever I'm ready, I can leave them behind.

I know that I don't know many things, that maybe I know nothing. I know that knowledge is invisible, at least when it's stored inside of me, which is the only time I know it actually works. I know how to talk when necessary. I know I can sing when I'm ready to.

I know that all music is true and that none of it is. Language works the same way. Something inside of both makes facts irrelevant: the sound of a voice echoing from deep within a new cave, scraping itself against something too enormous to see, something it might never find again, something I am invited to look at while it's there.

Music invites me to believe it, but I don't have to.

It offers its *I* like an outstretched hand, and I take it.

I roll down the windows, encouraged.

I sing.

II

I wish I still believed
every song was worth listening to
On my twenty-eighth birthday
I drew a circle around my body
indicating how deep my curiosity went
for things like space, the ocean, & facts
about multi-national corporations
I was embraced by the world
when I stopped trying to figure it out
& I slept in this embrace for weeks, for months
I still look for things in the sky
but I can't remember
who first asked me to do this
What I am presenting to you now
are hundreds of blueprints
for the creative rearrangement
of twenty-six bricks
There is a void in the wind
we can't stop singing at
I know the bees eat it
I don't really know how come

At the coffee shop I am listening
to two people explain to each other
how shitty the other one is being
The man keeps using the word *unpack*
The woman shakes her head
like it's still covered in earth
I want to love people
who love arguing about time
& what time does to them
& what time could never fix
One time I startled a young male elk
exiting a hot spring in Yellowstone
It was winter & neither of us
belonged where we were
I was naked in a way
that I'd like to go back to
Now I'm just new ink
in a new place
on the same gigantic arm
I can't tell if I'm stupid
or if Earth is a joke I don't get
Many animals will never be beloved
The ones with wild smells
that have nothing to do with people
The secret to pollen

is that it fucks everybody up
& then disappears into
beautiful things that keep us alive
My deprivation fantasies
all end the same way
My throat being too dry
& the sky too big
to swallow anyway

All winter I am thinking of gates
They open toward a summer
of friendly, sexless masses
I feel this capacity in me
like a showroom
full of bright mean lights
growing strange, victorious plants
I believe in space, I say to my neighbor
He slams the door on my nasturtiums
American Bravery is choosing
one pleasant evening
to lower gently into your blood
Wanting to know the world's secrets
without making the world uncomfortable
Meanwhile
morning plays the same old records
What are you talking about
it goes, & I go
out into it
with a fantastic invented memory
of the desert moon

People think beauty is something
that should count for or against you
The beauty that reveals itself to others
only in its excess
I jangle my beautiful coins
in my pocket for you
because all survival depends on making
the appropriate noises at the appropriate times
City planners prepare us for this
daily, silently
The tallest man in your memory
claims that the development
of modern agricultural practices
has led us into this great wide meadow
of men & women exercising their preferences
for one color palette over another
You believe him the way you believe
that in Central America
everyone sleeps in hammocks
alongside warm bodies of water
Information doesn't need to be true
to grow itself in your body like a peach
& be given as food to whoever, much later
What the world is
is making currency

from an ever-expanding meaningfulness
that carries no weight
You eat from it constantly
You can't carry it when you leave

There are six billion types
of infrastructure in this world
& everyone needs to be held
Mom wants to talk
about the condo plague
but only in the context
of the possession-as-idea
A foreman lifting his eyes
to reveal his very political tears
The body seeking solace
in the illusions of self-relief
There are no American poems
if you never leave America
or if you forget that a concept
can never truly be named
Behind the people I love
are the people they failed at loving
I am out in the yard again
knifing at the seams of it
with my hands

The rite of the young girl
is embarrassing herself
& then the task of the woman
is choosing an embarrassment
she could live inside forever
When I transcend cars
it will be for a walking that pains me
One that polishes the grass stains
on my bare legs & feet
I will need you then, shoeless in Austin
I will need your ponytail to be real
& existing only for itself
When I drive across
that cracked wide freeway
over the Mississippi—what will I need then?
Everything's harmless
from up on this motorcycle
We go to the river together
on the Internet
every day

No one talks about the number of times
they've said to a near-stranger
I've never felt this way about anyone
The way we remember
to choose vegetables, or which colors
look best against our skin
is not actual memory
Actual memory is stored in the body
You forget breathing
when you open the memory back up for air
When you get to the island
you'll have to cut a path
through a thick, colorful fog
It feels like growing
when there is nowhere good
to grow into

It took me two decades
to respect powerpop as a physical force
Now it lives in me like a great Christmas
People change
I am asleep in my childhood bedroom
or else I am pretending to be asleep
in my childhood itself
In your twenties
you feel so violently
about whatever peace means
You are a woman so naked
no one bothers to figure out why
People ask me how I am doing
like it's impossible to feel excitement
at being blown apart
There is no peace in this world
like a shitload of meaning
or in aching for something
whose word doesn't exist
The pale blue heaven
of Nebraska
What happens to my legs
when he begins to drum

Certain kinds of talk
are good for all kinds of weather
My man bought a big book
on growing psilocybin
& we are disturbed at the frequency
with which lab equipment appears
Exactness—*what now?*
I can't hear you
under the weight of all this foliage
The shape of my life
is a billowing-enough dress
that renders the body beneath it
wholly mysterious
Do not come around me
just to discuss your skeleton
It's pineapple season
& I am very much in love

At the beach, two old women
suggest we buy the country store
What do I look like I asked
as they grip my long black hair
What can I say about that young girl
in the sand, flying the kite
of her little round belly
beneath the country's dying gaze?
That women are always caught
in a state of performance
or behind the glass case
of their own magnificent limbs?
There is no way to talk about
her pale pink sports bra
without the moment caving in
to an exterior fantasy
So I won't
I drop the diamond of her body
into the lake of my body
I concentrate very hard
on turning the ripples into waves

New Spiritualism
is listening to Rumours
going, *Did you hear what she said?*
I want a man to explain
why we murder our great sages
by categorizing them as soft rock
You can feel anything for four minutes
is how I walk through this person-forest
kissing everyone on the neck
To re-live the Golden Moments
you need a thing to measure
& a thing to write the measurement down
You need a big thing to remember you
when you are gone
I've never understood
why anyone would need that

There's a kind of art
in losing track of yourself
Returning to the mossy rocks
where the pit of you was shaped
You lay in bed at night
& notice you are featureless
That everything is in the midst
of becoming itself
& then changes its mind
Yellowed horses in the American desert
galloping endlessly for a community
we refuse to include
I see you wanting to photograph it
so I photograph it
A very expensive memory
where a meadow used to be

On the radio the men are talking
about music as an institution
of individual power
Actually
they are introducing me
to the nineteen-year-old girl
as Brand New Spectacle of Wealth
I am in a strip mall in Sacramento
locating myself inside the pyramid
of American Visibility
Singing is listed in the manual
as conducive to energetic sensation
The purpose of a song
is giving direction
or insisting that others
repeat your thoughts outloud
I strap it on & give it a try
A power I was born deficient of
floods through me like milk
I wrestle something out of my mouth
& give it a little listen
I'm not sure I understand it
but look, now—
there it goes

There is a certain something in a man's face
but I still regret that we are encouraged to look for it
Dad says making money
means one fixer-upper after another
but I think that's just being alive
What kind of a person prioritizes Love
& not just hardening into a single gender
in tiny, embarrassing increments?
I want to be them
I want a job
that leaks slowly into a lake
& I want to swim in this lake my whole life
I regret that too
The couple next to me
punctures the air with their graduate degrees
The West Coast is so insular he says
& huge animals start to fuck in my stomach
Some people are born into a detachment
that lays across their lifespan
like wilting lavender
but I am still grateful
I am grateful for these moments
when I am all alone with my thoughts
& letting them stream out of me
I am grateful for those beaming men
who just want to tell us
everything they know

Sincere, unsolicited advice
is the worst kind of burden
For instance, practice hardening
into the You you are
despite the external influences
of your family or friends
I never cared about Bonsai trees
conceptually & now I am ready
to internalize this very specific pain
All life would ask of me
is to shrink to a more manageable size
& demand a strict schedule of watering
Root beer floats
in the redwood forest
Long walks toward the center of me
flowering with new guilts
Don't be so hard on yourself, you offer
& I practice the version of me
that knows exactly what you mean

If you are in love, spend the money
on a split-headphones jack
You can get them cheaply
at any major airport or cinema
& the rest of us crave this symbol
I'm somewhere in the Sky Mall
fetishizing my relationship with pets
I'm having a renaissance with myself
& the big woman next to me
She feels so soft I ask
for two complimentary beverages
& that's just it / *permission is easy*
If the world is the parking lot
or if the world is the mall
the teenagers inside us
still work for somebody else
When we listen to Pink Floyd
I can feel it being meaningful
My secrets becoming a currency
My light shows
increasingly private

Every trick to remaining porous
involves a freeway
The freeway is mostly endless
fields of hot concrete littered with police
& this is where the holes come in
Anthems of disobedience
nurturing less-popular sectors of the economy
Midwestern teenagers smoking weed
through each other's limp blonde hair
If I grow into a woman I'd like it to feel
like a heated pan slowly cooling
against my beloved's cheek
Like scratching the paint off a fingernail
with a different fingernail
I remember to remember
that every version of me
is scale-modeled after a better me
Better Me, please do not internalize
the fear that people pass off as sensibility
Just because it's a rite of passage
doesn't mean it's a good idea

People never get tired
of hearing the most obvious things
Love is indescribable
burns straight up the charts
& rains itself down on us over & over again
The effect of production is startling
in its ability to make others think *that's easy*
Really, we are all too far gone
down our own specific tunnels to act
I didn't exist & then I was born
something is saying
Something getting piped in
from a warred-over reservoir
that probably isn't even worth
walking up to
In order to connect with others
you have to practice believing their moods
Start with your favorite popular musician
They have a small set of complicated desires
They are highly motivated
to get what they deserve

I'm boarding the plane
with the other American mystics
I'm eating dried apples & watching their news
There are feelings in the air here
I can't recognize
A girl with white hair
touching the sides of her short white neck
Back in Phoenix / Big Blank Epiphany
Children & grandparents
wearing scarves as a joke
One person gives another person
the plain gift of cold soda
& all our militaries advance
I'm charging my electronics
in my own little corner
of this cemetery
If everything was really okay
I don't think we'd need
to remind ourselves

In the grocery store
I can never make a decision
A single light in a detached garage
or the cultural benefits
of popular consumption
Parents beg you to participate
because this is their right
This is a fluorescent first aid kit
to them & they are correct
There are several ways to interpret
a person's love of medicine
but this is not why I am here
I am buying two white onions
for the person I love
who is at home wondering
what has taken me so long

Knowing that time heals all
doesn't heal you at all
This is a joke we made up
while spinning the chakra wheels
from Self to Sex to Power
I watch you walk in the warm street
& it doesn't matter whose arms
you are allowing into you
It's spring is a great excuse
Like painting your bedroom
the color of an older bedroom
for the sake of your championship
We go into the forest
because the forest is full
of useless self-knowledge
like what to do with your hands
when you are high
Like how to turn loneliness
into intelligence
The way water in a clear jar
becomes something else
when left by the bed overnight
Life can't be that hard
if this many people are alive
The deer can be a nuisance

but some nights it's nice
just to hear something moving

There's a pool in me I can't evaporate
Big blank face in the white sun
I walked through the Joshua trees
with plastic bags through my fingers
& a bad song in my mind
The badness of which I measured
by its inability to move my body
away from its own predispositions
There have been so many times
I have been so afraid of the world
How it only ever teaches you
Medicine, Commerce, Walking Upright
We let teenagers onto the planet
hoping they choose to grow older
& fix something
We let violence come into us
hoping it chooses to grow soft
with context & be fixed
I walked farthest when I was lonely
& the blood streaming from me
became a kind of graph
The flowers of Earth
are full of information
Sometimes you are looking at them
Other times they're just there

Once I read a short story
about a woman playing Nintendo
alone in the desert
The rest I don't remember
though I keep a fictionalized vision
of her hair in my mind
At the time, I was so indignant
I sat in a bright swimming pool
near the Mexican border
nursing my alienation
into a potent psychedelic
As far as advice goes:
Let your self-righteousness
billow into a parachute—*Why not?*
Listen to old songs
about Los Angeles, knowing
what is too painful to ever actually know
There will never be an appropriate context
to explain to the person you love
that in many ways
they are better off without you
Let them discover it in your absence
& your body will split effortlessly
One gallon
of clean drinking water
A bright, skinless orange
in your palm

No one brings their Corgi out
until it's good & hot
I eat the lemon popsicle of my mind
in the park with all the Youngs
Living things have always been accessories
or even jokes, I remember
The juice runs down the elbow
& becomes part of the grass
I'd like to know what comes
after the disavowal of illusions
but before the final severance
The city is expensive, & yet
to experience the city costs nothing
It gets boring
hauling around a narrative
of utter powerlessness
or of the way our public spaces
used to really *gleam*
History & Culture are rich
with the means of escape
but you can take it or leave it
The battlefields of this wild country
always ending up in your air

All day I waited for the photographer
to write me back: amethyst, quartz, or citrine?
He's a minimalist, I swoon into the river
& the water fans the tiny flame
We didn't feel like going to the beach
We got our nails painted
& said a few things about space
The truth is, I roll in the surf
of this being over
All weekend long
we whined on the tracks of ourselves
& you still owe me money
I have nowhere to be in the morning
so life is glorious again
like it was in the beginning
New, alone, depressed, lost, starving
Thank you for changing everything
Sitting with me in the river
Listening to it go

At the tire shop, all the mechanics
are mispronouncing Klonopin
A morning show host debunks agave
behind an array of processed grain products
I text you: *It is so wonderful that we persevere*
in selling the ultimate shopping experience
& increasingly complicated versions of feeling safe
You text me back: GO OUTSIDE
When you have love
you zip yourself inside it like a tent
You watch everything outside the tent
smear itself together seamlessly
Direct sunlight, the shadows of leaves
A person you are no longer afraid
of turning into
On the way to work
at long last, I see a man kneeling
before a section of wet concrete
with his fingers on his chin
I want to talk to you about language
& this needs a new kind of language
That flowering, eternal darkness
we don't have to look at anymore

Almost every method of preparation
is only preparing you
for your eventual disappointment
A woman in my apartment building told me this
as a way of convincing me to leave Los Angeles
I sat like potted aloe in her apartment
eating grapes with that moment
when you realize what you must do
& don't think you can
We have been trained to recognize
the signs of our own body's deterioration
through its brilliant walls
We let Culturally Persuasive Medias
command us toward an enjoyment of life
that more closely resembles
a positive economic correlation
All this to say
I rode my bicycle home over the wet streets
I repeated your name in the dark
I felt certain that anything could be eaten
& only its beauty digested
Those paintings made sense to me
suddenly, completely
Lying with you on some moss
& then again on some different moss

We were kissing by the water
& there were no commercials
The moon looked so sick
I know I know
I'm doing a terrible job of explaining it
But I noticed you, building a fire
& in the morning, how you slept
& during the day
the way you walked

Before I knew how to be touched
I used to want to live on an island
I was constructing this island
in the South Pacific
using blasting techniques
& tens of thousands of sandbags of fear
In a dream or something
I moved through a marketplace
The idea of Morocco
shone from each woven basket
while Actual Morocco just laid there existing
like an unwaxed piece of fruit
waiting to lose the sense of importance
I used to want to feel for it
but never really could
The evidence suggests
it was all worth it in the end
How do you photograph a mountain
without it breaking someone's heart

When you are young
every devastation is an opportunity
Your bare feet flowering
on whole beds of black mold
Extended families show up
in your dreams to tell you
how time has mangled their bodies
& to convince you that the dark pocket
of their own travesty is unique
This is not true
When you are young, you have no choice
but to be devastated
& no one will ever explain
that you will be unwanted until you are grown
That you will be unwanted after that too
but for a different reason
The opportunity is in the ability
of your mind to forget its deprivations
It takes courage to acknowledge
just how easy it is
to become lost

Nothing says Impermanence
like a bouquet of wildflowers
from the grocery store
That & when sports arenas
are mercilessly drained of their people-blood
with three whole minutes left to play
Doesn't it hurt their feelings?
You will know immediately
what kind of man he is
when the credits begin to roll
& he sits waiting in the dark theater
For what?
I'm out for a walk now
with all of my arguments
I like to leave them
on curbs, or old staircases
Places where the leaves pile up
Where children aren't likely
to get a hold of them

Beautiful Southwestern towns
are insulated in their degradation
by a very expensive charm
One person makes history
by making whole swaths of men
incredibly uncomfortable
Georgia O'Keeffe
painting deserts & mountains
beneath her big black hat
says *hold on just one moment*
into a horizon of wincing towers
This is how we remember her
Strolling through
our planned communities
Waiting for somebody
to knock out our wind

At long last I am going to hell
but not the one we know how to talk about
I am riding a thunderbolt
of big-sister feelings
down a quiet, suburban street
It's a slow leak says the bicyclist
but he can't seem to find the nail
He puts the whole thing underwater
& says something about the wound
I think Holiness is possible
The Holiness of being blown apart
& making peace with your lost limbs
What are you up to says the bicyclist
but I guess you had to be there
I go walking through the rhododendrons
because I love the way it sounds

Where is the Tennessee Valley Authority
now that we have Los Angeles?
Some people cut the road into the mountain
& some people just walk along it
singing about it
Impermeable surfaces are where we keep
our understanding of how we suffer
We remedy our suffering
by first learning to recognize
the parts that hurt the most
when rubbed up against it
Federal Work Programs also built pools
Miles & miles of cavernous pools
White snakes in the desert
& bottomless as sand
I ache for them, even as I swim around
There are just so many other parts
I can't also be

I love my dad so much it makes me cry
He is deep in the fortress of himself
watching me construct my own
There are so many years
where you don't have a hand to hold
& this is when you develop your badness
Once I taught fifth graders about soil cycles
in the woods of rural Pennsylvania
It got dark & a few of them
had only some sweatpants
Had never seen bears
Drank soda & ate chips
so gracefully, as if no edges could catch
on the pink gum of their insides
What I was afraid of
I was also enamored with
An understanding of resources
that pressed my cheek to the empathy fire
The world is punishment enough
in that you see everything lying there
but have no agency to rearrange it
You have to build a tiny city
in your mind then
full of constructed emergencies
you will one day know
how to prepare for

I pulled a stray hair from my mouth
during our luminous breakfast
No one is God but me
I noticed you dancing at night
off & on, for several years
When you stopped, I was still attending
to the buying & selling of vehicles
You said your heart
was a swimming pool back then
You stretched a bright blue tarp
so carefully over its surface
when the leaves started to roll in
Leaves? I asked
What an engaging thing to protect
I think of my grandmother
in her floral bathing suit
Scooping out frogs with her clean net
Almost always you tell me
& I gaze into the future
where my body is so beautiful
but no longer belongs to me

So many women make my guts unfurl
like great pale flags on the White House lawn
People say *burning* like it's no big thing
but then your limbs begin failing
before you can read the instructions
Listen to the words!
Men & women with ancient hair
have been screaming for decades
about the downfall of society
& this is how I know
we are all going to be just fine
Feeling guilty for your inability
is feeling angry at my inability
& no fruit grows there
I'd like to give you permission
to feel something else altogether
Reverence for the multitude
of your own wranglings
Warm muscles after a deep snow

I liked it in the early nineties
when bands would hand-draw
their own cassette tape sleeves
Really, there is no one to impress
I like when people remind me
of my imminent disintegration
without trying to convince me
of what it will look like
Old women with long gray hair
& butterfly tattoos on their ankles
Not to mention the canyons of Utah
that demand nothing of us
Not even that we all go home
Everyone Struggles
is the cliché that everyone forgets
Morning, do not laugh at me
Every time you come around
I am still not quite myself

One lengthy article
about managing expectations
& ten thousand pictures
of naked women in pastels
God put me in charge
of whistleblowing but
there's no percussion in a hymn
I count the apples in every liquor store
& other than that, I'm aimless
The Blood Moon changed me
The Supermoon ate me out
I give me permission
to bail on whatever
That's why I'm still in love

Ancient records deny nothing
but agree that no one reads
I write on my napkin *I am blessed to be alive!*
& walk my whole body into the filing cabinet
of a completely unreasonable decade
Small pleasures, including incense
were found lining the walls of the tomb
The great men paid to finger them
tipped their hats to a mystery
they still could not afford—
Does that help?
I watch my generation get fucked
against the walls of clever speech
& still intend a whole religion
of Learning How to Care
I feel for the hair of them
in this weird, warm dark
Burning the kind
that invites the spirits back in

I am in the railyard of my mind
with the possessions of my childhood
There is a man eyeing me
from across the yard
because he knows this metaphor
& he doesn't trust me to take care of it
When we become holy
every song is a cliché
I don't know the word for it
I just like the way it looks
When he tunes his guitar at last
When he starts in
with the harmonica
& the girl he loves
joins him at the chorus
Know what I mean?
A river couldn't just die
but it's gone now too
I am fumbling my body
into a beautiful epiphany
Helpless, helpless,
helpless, he is singing
& we are going
yeah

III

The summer after graduating college, my best friend and I moved onto a small farm in the remote mountains of Northern California. The American Economy had just collapsed, and with the possibility of entering the job market removed from the table, we decided to dedicate that summer to the performance art piece of Sacred Irresponsible Experience.

We packed our books, clothing, and art supplies into the trunk of my car and drove north from San Francisco into the remote hills of Humboldt County, ready to shape our lives around what we envisioned to be a kind of off-grid utopia—falling asleep to the white noise of generators, hardening into the sort of peaceful revolutionaries we believed should inherit the earth.

We arrived with an earnestness I can now just barely recognize. We took pictures of the tops of trees. The sky was wild there—a gradient blue that encouraged weather without ever actually hosting any. We were welcomed by a weird kinship of builders who pointed out the creek and instructed us to make ourselves at home.

We were being paid, it seemed, to plug several metaphysical holes in the scene. I say this because we had very few important tasks, and we were encouraged to take our time with the ones we did have—weeding around forgotten tool sheds, picking blackberries for The Boys, things like that. During our lunch breaks we scratched down our thoughts, or stretched out smoking with the other workers on the deck. We rode four-wheelers up the long logging roads to the greenhouses in our sports bras, watering the plants for whole days, alone.

In our free time we tried our best to continue with what we had tasked ourselves with throughout our school years: researching the world in an attempt to understand and improve upon it. We read books by dead philosophers and living musicians, dated newspaper articles about civil wars on other continents. *What can we do*, we wondered, though everything seemed to be working out fine. Translucent weeks went by. We tallied our earnings and spun our wheels.

It was confusing, mostly. I was twenty-two years old and couldn't understand that part of being an employee was learning how to skillfully kill time. I sat in the same sun every morning—reading other people's big thoughts, letting them blow me apart—and then I made a sandwich and headed up the hill, unsure of where any of us were going.

What can we do, I needed to know. There in that warm valley, two hours from the nearest post office, I wondered if I would ever be asked to do anything. Elsewhere, everywhere, the country was deteriorating. I watched from the safety of Relative Comfort, learning how the world actually worked.

We were lonely, disoriented, completely at peace. Four colors to the landscape, no phone service for miles. With all the distractions of life removed, what we were left with was the responsibility of deciding what life actually was.

Through this wild field, it helped to create a trail.

Our trail was a daily routine—a fairly simple, fairly common kind of trail to build. We made our coffee; we drank it on the deck; we took a few notes; we went to work. We had a little cabin to ourselves, a cobwebbed outbuilding with a sleeper sofa and someone's mom's old TV. Every night we made a fire, and when the fire died out we would cross back through the dark field with our single flashlight to read or paint a little, eventually falling into an empty sleep.

I don't know if rituals are created out of a kind of neurotic loneliness or if it's the other way around. I know our days collapsed into themselves, into several other days, which is how time functions when you are lost or comfortable. Throughout history, humans have introduced new species of plants and animals to a barren landscape, just to see what would happen. At one point it was Eucalyptus. Now, generally, it's media.

The Last Waltz is a music film, Martin Scorsese's 1978 documentary about The Band's farewell show. It's a concert film, really, a commemoration of sixteen years of touring and writing songs. More importantly, it was the only movie we had to watch, and against that soundless backdrop of rural American asceticism, it became the only thing capable of absorbing our angst.

We started putting the movie on as we made breakfast in the morning, letting it play each night until we fell asleep.

We developed unique and voyeuristic relationships with each member of The Band, with their cast of friends and musical guests: Neil Young, Joni Mitchell, Eric Clapton, Muddy Waters, Bob Dylan. We watched open-mouthed at Van Morrison's ecstatic high kicks and sequined pants, at Mavis Staples channeling God in gold hoops. We let ourselves into their vision, relieved of the responsibility of creating our own. We made ourselves at home within their music, which is exactly what art invites.

I can't say what other people are looking for when they watch films, or what they are listening for when they hear music. What I think I found in that film was a resonance, a validation. The offering of an outstretched hand. I was lost, then, in that open field of fear—the one you live in before you can admit to yourself the difference between what your life is and what it might be. Before you begin to move toward it. Before you know how to begin at all.

Music, for me, provided a beginning. I studied the creased faces under the hot lights, I watched them move and smile and shake their instruments. There was no distance between their bodies and the sounds that streamed out of them. They weren't afraid of me, or the countless others watching. They ate my watching them out of the air.

Here is how a song begins: its sound punctures a quiet room cleanly and then it continues on in confidence, in absolute trust of its own right to exist. You recognize and celebrate its entrance into the world, its immediate demand to take up space. You sing along, learning.

What I learned from them was how to begin, whether I wanted to or not. How to begin thinking about beginning, removed from the machinery of the rest of the world, from my ideas of how the world actually functioned, which were, mostly, completely wrong. To begin to envision what life could be and how to enter it, nudged onward by the evidence of life in others, by the joy on their faces, in the sound of their own clear voices pronouncing what they knew to be True.

That September, we got kicked off the farm. We headed north with our belongings, packing the movie along with us. We watched it from the carpeted floor of our empty house in Portland, blowing gently on the tiny flame of any joy we had previously earned. Our money had run out by then, and so had the country's. We cried on the broken front porch, unemployed and directionless, while Richard Manuel sang from the kitchen: *Go out yonder, peace in the valley / Come downtown, have to rumble in the alley / Oh, you don't know the shape I'm in.*

I don't know how or why these words continue to affect me; I don't know if I actually know what they mean. The *Shape*. I mean, I know what they mean to me. If they could make me feel what I feel, what I felt, the words must be irrelevant.

Most of the time the way we feel doesn't have a corresponding word. It takes a whole clump of them, set to a rhythm, coming out of a specific mouth, to make themselves understood. From that landscape, from that place in my life, and from those mouths, I heard something that made sense. Helplessness, Joy. I haven't heard anything like it since.

Now when I listen to The Band, I hear a dull echo of what I once felt so acutely— that awful and glorious weight of knowing exactly what kind of sublimity is possible in the world while, simultaneously, having absolutely no power to achieve it. I think of that time, and the time right after, when we were both blown our separate ways, bullied into years of hopelessness by an economic system that none of us have any control over. I think of those years and it makes me cry. Still: I listen.

I wonder why this is, but then again I already know. We return to the sites of our own demolition, just to remember—*what?* That we lived through it? That we live, in general?

I return because I learn from it, from the yearning and the isolation. I learn from diving into my own desperate fissures, my fucked up and oily seas. I learn from watching others do the same thing. As best we can, we document our self-navigation. If we're lucky, our map helps someone else along their way.

I return because, increasingly, I do not recognize the world into which I was born, and into which I have no choice but to grow. More and more, Popular Music seems to represent the affirmation of and participation in a fictional and destructive machine—outside of me entirely, commanding me to get going. When I believe this world, I am able to listen. When I return to the old voices, it's because I can't believe what the world has become.

But still, I return. I return to the unbelievable world.

I return to locate my body inside it, in gratitude and disbelief that it could continue on.

I return to what I'm learning, or to what I haven't yet learned. I return to what I think I've learned and I practice un-learning it.

Mostly, I return to listen. Sometimes this takes years. I return to it in isolation or in happiness—I wait quietly for the full fire of it to be lit before me.

That you have to remove yourself from the world in order to truly see it is so simple and lonely and true.

How beautiful that we yearn to do this.

That afterward, we return to sing.

IV

When my dream cloud got punctured
I cried realistically
When I made a familiar sound
I got critically acclaimed
Casual Thoughtlessness
is so pervasive
that now I'm invested
I hold my breath & watch it
move through the world
all on its own

All my friends
are moving to Los Angeles
She's a fascist, says the Goodwill clerk
& hands me a new book
Wanting to learn a thing or two
is a dangerous position to be in
Girls just wanna have fun
says the loudspeaker
& the people swing
their brightly colored arms

Looking at the lives of others qualifies as a pastime
At the grocery store, I think: *gum?*
I multiply all the gas stations I can think of
by two to four bunches of just-freckling bananas
Harm me, I feel like
I must be whispering

Oregon has cold beaches
Washington has rocky islands
California has those freeway ribbons
& the softest kind of thoughts
I thought it was impossible
to give up on a dream this slowly
Stevie Nicks makes me feel so unimportant
though I can't really imagine
feeling anything else

Music is a bad hologram
of a very important memory
I am climbing a new mountain
called Reverence For God
It is making me a woman
I just can't seem
to learn

You write to me about a new photographer
I write back: *That mountain!*
This, truly, could be enough
This, & the birthmark on your stomach
you still don't know how to work around

The elevated mind does not need to speak
We are at the airport again, the
elevated airport, & being careful
I have an idea, one of us says
We keep walking in silence
past a bright kiosk of cinnamon rolls

Wanting to be of service
is also a kind of service
I do a handstand in the gravel
because I know you need some help
I find a hole in the ground
filled with sad Neil Young songs
Tiny yellow flowers
on the sloped lawns
of the mind

All suffering becomes uninteresting
the moment you acclimate
to how much it hurts
Once I walked into a field
because I believed in the field
When I finally became the field
people were always leaving
somewhere through me

The opposite of fear
is another kind of fear
A perceived scarcity
that moves the country's blood
The card I drew said *Sacrifice*
is the act of making sacred
The evidence is everywhere
Three kinds of chimes
in a bitter wind

The mind will convince the body
to endure more pain than it should
Magazines
& women reading magazines
The partial list of distractions
includes Mechanization
& Team Sports
What are we being trained for
if not things like this

I'm in a museum
& I'm thinking
Great works of art will never change
unless they are looked at for too long
I'm kidding!
I'm not in a museum
I'm watching three American tourists
take pictures of me at work

Cultural events
do not make demands
for their own relevancy
We do that
We do that

The best fantasy sport
is Intellectualized Feeling
versus Biological Response
You drank a forty on the beach
& now you're someone else
A ten-year-old girl
flying a kite in her swimsuit
A twelve-year-old girl
making her swimsuit
a kite

Image will replace speech
& then convince speech
that this is language's fault
Now you know how I feel
riding my bike through a neighborhood
I will never be able to afford

Participation & dissipation
is the cycle on which to locate the body
Perception & deception
Proration & deterioration
The Buddhists maintain
their position on labels
Two flowers
might as well be one thousand

We make a practice
of attempting to describe water
We photograph a mountain
but it never really turns out
When I learn something about myself
I pitch a small rock into a river
Only other people's songs
feel weightless
& true

In the metropolis we argue
about who feels loneliness more acutely
In the desert we are together
& lighting as many fires as we want
You don't need anyone's permission
to build it up / to get it going
All art is a war of volume
Be careful
not to lose your voice

When you buy a truck you are actually buying
everything you'd like it to haul
The bed is so empty
I have begun to hallucinate
My money moves around
like a bad rag on a kitchen table:
House plants are expensive
but then again

Being rich does not require you
to be smart or kind
but everyone wants to be rich
Jet boats gleaming
and then beginning to speak
I am proud of you, brother
though not un-worried, either
Moving through
this long life
in love

Humans would benefit greatly
from daily interactions
with predatory animals
(Somewhere, an Institution
perks up its million ears)

Insert Powerful Optimism!
you write to me
after the too-long car ride
of holding down a job
An authority figure is speaking
& I am encouraged to listen
Now I have
this whole list of questions
that I'm too embarrassed
to not be asking anymore

The most lucrative industries
facilitate the misrepresentation
of your digital self
Photographs of water
Photographs of trees
I'd like to be purposeless
with a little specificity
The exact person I was born as
but older

I'd like a barbaric explanation
of the Gregorian calendar
that takes five minutes or less
I'd like a few more friends
who were comfortable telling me the truth
I swam naked in a lake once
& wild animals watched me
Everything could make me bigger
is what I'm trying to say

There's dust in the healing hut
Black spiders
with bodies like grapes
I write in my diary
Utopia is not sustainable
& assume that everyone agrees
I know you know
we need a new national anthem
Sometimes I feel like
all I do is look

When the earthquake hits:
glass & money &
several hundred thousand identities
You scrambled over the wall
of something immense to arrive here
The Wall is what's real
Here, there are only cafés

Resource maps are so confrontational
Peak Oil is so 2008
It makes sense
that everything is so fucked up
Think about the way you felt
before you found
your one true love

There is recognizing the man
in the pink sweater
& then there is recognizing
yourself in this man
Either way, there is recognition
Either way, you have done
nothing wrong

When you grow up in the countryside
you get big ideas about space
I thought the desert was a spectacle
but the epilogue was off
I think Las Vegas
is the most uninteresting
kind of empty there is
I'm only in the backseat
because I want to go for a ride

America for Americans
is for almost Anyone Else
A sign is most powerful
when it is a little difficult to read
You scroll through a phone
& here come the new mysteries
What am I supposed to do?
one wonders, & the work week
gets born all over again

If it's a full moon tonight
I won't have to wonder
when the full moon will be back
I won't have to gyrate
beneath a paid-for glow
The Contemporary Job Market
is 10,000 variations
of sifting through dead information
My God, what we could impregnate
with all this actual blood

All art dies
by its own gentrification
Many of us are cowards
but not all

No one expects you
not to self-define
by negation
I came to her in tears
in 2010 / in the evening
No one will tell you
what true money means
but you can feel for it
Out in the yard
with the city's jasmine
Gazing & gazing
at an enormous
& necessary machine

Improving upon language
is so embarrassing
Solving the language problem
is hallucinatory at best
I'm in the frozen foods aisle
& it's raining
I am the only president
of whatever it is I've built

There's a new mood now
the whole neighborhood's in
Elections are so rigged
we talk about it at the grocery store
I spit on cops
all day in my mind
All I wanna do
is have a little fun
before I die

In my dream a big woman
says *Fuck with language*
Another woman says *No*
Hold it in this tiny shell
I know skin is beautiful
I know paintings of ravens
are beautiful
I eat cold white rice
from yesterday
Worried that I'll lose
my ached-for thing

All the news outlets
watch all the other news outlets
A plant can't quite learn
how to water itself

Glazed-over animosity
gets the best spot in the showroom
I cleaned off in the river
I have never felt so calm in my life
There is smoke from the fire
but I didn't start the fire
but it's *in* me
I know there is nothing outside
of the smell of your mouth
in the morning
But still

Every day my True Love
scars himself with fantasy
A large framed photograph
of a plentiful source of water
When boundaries become meaningless
I will eat the death pill
with him in my arms
Have something
to show for your suffering
Life is too long
to never need help

Only women own blood enough
to each month let some go
I know why we don't want
to walk in the woods
The woods are
[makes engulfing motion with arms]

Technology is boring
but not as boring
as our addiction to technology
The thing about people is
they force you to have an opinion
I go walking in nature
I try to let it become me
Children with ideas:
Do not waste your time
talking to adults

If everyone sees themselves
in the sky
the sky is a sham
A man carries a guitar case
across a major intersection
filled with god knows what
When he sings a song to me
I wait for his name
to hide itself in my body
If it doesn't, the song is worthless
If it does, we can move on
to Familiar Childhood Medias

Missing the ghosts of yourself
is missing the child
who still recognizes them
If you eat the shellfish
& you are still hungry
load a different kind
of language into the gun

There is nothing inside of you
that hasn't been invited
There is no part of your body
you didn't once choose to eat
You are asking me to lead you
to the rocks where you will perish
Vote With Your Dollars
sounds about right

What pushes us upward toward the divine
is always at the mercy of the colony
6" Tropical Plant, $24.99
I cried all night
& I don't feel like talking about it

The great Dream of our age
is to love what you are paid for
The great Myth of our age
is that this happens how we want
The children of America
do not need our sleeplessness
You bore them
into an evaporating marsh
They know how incredible
your love must be

How do you stop gods
from getting stuck in your skin?
I sing their hymns
just to keep them at bay
Tanya Tucker
in her sad little Brooklyn apartment
chooses Open Field over Winding Trail
How come I know this?
There is a balm that soothes me
but it has since been discontinued
Other than that
it just helps to talk

V

I have this memory of being young.

I'm in the passenger seat of my dad's pickup truck and I am asking for something.

I am begging, really, though I can't remember what for—a toy, maybe, or new clothes. We are on our way to school, or else coming back from school. I can't remember that either.

What I remember is the asking: the kind of naked fear it brings. I am getting desperate now, swinging the dull blade of language, overwhelmed by the agony of potentially being denied.

But my dad is watching me, smiling, so I have hope. The fog lifts from the bay as we drive alongside it. When he opens his mouth to respond, I prepare to dissolve in joy. What I actually remember is feeling confused.

He is singing, I realize: a kind of rough, swooping chant. *You can't always get what you want*, he sings, still smiling at me calmly. He makes an easy little tune of it, with the *can't* and the *get* and the *want* accentuated. He even laughs a little while he does it, tapping his fingers on the wheel.

For months this song would come back, so frequently that I came to expect it in place of a definitive answer. *You can't always get what you want*, he sang—sugar cereal, a tape player, skipping school. I thought he was making fun of me—of my discomfort with wanting something, or of my powerlessness to get it in the first place. After a while I learned how not to ask.

Years later, while listening to the radio at a friend's house, I was informed by a local disc jockey that this refrain did not come from my father; that in fact it was the chorus to a song written by a popular English rock band called the Rolling Stones. I sat on the floor of her parents' living room, head cocked, listening to that pitching man's voice singing at the whole world, feeling a thick cloud in me begin to slowly come apart.

I felt initiated into a new language, or the opportunity for a new language to exist. I felt the weight of the softest punishment being released at last. *You can't always get what you want.* It was so *true.*

Those moments when our own small worlds are punctured, when the new air comes streaming in—*who are we then?* What are the words for those moments, for the way we understand them wholly, before we reach (again) for a handrail in the dark, before we begin (again) to smooth pure Experience into mere Information.

You can't always get what you want. It made me happy, somehow. Rinsed and validated by the radio, I understood it at once. It wasn't just me being denied, it was the whole world—everyone listening, everyone who had ever listened. We were all being denied, all of us, and my dad too.

I suspect that this is what music is for, or at least that this is what we ask music to do. To create an arena for the facilitation of human connection, to bind us together in something that we would otherwise never push ourselves to describe.

Music makes space for us, entire continents of space. It provides us with new languages and images with which to describe it to one another, new emotional esthetics with which to interpret the experience of Living. It even provides us with a person to which we can outsource the interpretation of this experience. Out of this mouth, our feelings flow.

You can't always get what you want. I am watching, and listening, for something meaningful. Up on stage, things glow and explode. Every eye tracks what's shining. I see the systems working, I see the logistics and the technology. I am patient.

I am listening for an explanation—how did this happen? How do you hold yourself in this tenuous space? What is the shape of happiness, and money? Where do I go, if not toward you?

Music is an idea given to millions of people at once. Popular ideas climb straight up the charts. What we believe in most sits at the top of a pyramid, laughing at us. When it doesn't mean anything, that means something too.

Music is sacred, remember? It yanks on our bodies like the

moon. When done correctly, it makes us cry. We offer ourselves to it, the way I wish we did with love.

You can't always get what you want. Who said that? I am combing old receipts for the evidence of What I Know. It is a pile of culture. I am patient.

Music is where we store our knowledge. We bury it there, all kinds. When we play it back we remember what we needed to internalize—our most obvious truths, the ones we could never really hear.

Does art tell us anything that we don't already know, or think we know; anything that doesn't remind us of something else, something we've already heard?

You can't always get what you want. Information floats through the decades alongside me, along with me, instantly recognizable, widely distributed, basically free. I lower my body into the stream. I am eager to learn.

I am eager to understand: what do I need to know? The world's leaves change colors and die. I lean on music to help me fumble through my own emotions, and then I fumble through them, and then I just am.

I am a naked human body in a stream of sound.

The sound has authority and charisma. Over and over, I give in.

I give in to the colors, the waves of noise.

I reach my hand out to touch something living, I give in.

I want the echo of life in my own ears, I want the words I've memorized in the mouth of another.

I am alone, I give in. Let me be in there with everyone else.

You can't always get what you want. Even now I am soothed by this song, by my recognition of it, though it has denied me my whole life. I can't hear the words; I don't want to hear them. I hear something I've heard before and this is enough.

You can't always get what you want. Is anyone listening?

I get older, I become lost, I drift away from the people I love.

I don't want to learn the country's languages; I don't want to see them devastate my life. Money, Politics, Power, War. Over and over, we stomach the Unreal. I want to know I don't have to.

Popular Music does not owe us this. It owes itself only its own popularity, which it maintains by telling people what it believes they should know.

What this is, is none of my business, though it's easy enough to listen and guess.

You can't always get what you want, the World insists, and always will.

Let's listen to something else, I say.

The moon shining in the dark, there, just above the trees.

VI

I have this memory
I don't know how to take care of
We are walking across the parking lot
of the Tucson Airport
with our hands threaded together
& tears streaming down my face

The metaphor of the desert
is nowhere near as lonely
as the desert itself
Gigantic, spined plants
hide their bodies in the dead hills
guarding their water like I did
I was dead then too
in the imprint of your living body
I didn't have the words
to disarm our suffering & I still don't
& now, America, you sweep the hair
from my neck while I cry

I do not believe
that I should be made to feel guilty
for the total disintegration
of your Original Truth
Or to be satisfied with metaphors

that resign the human body
to a single function
within a more complicated series
of functions

But I am here

We walked to the reservoir
in the late afternoon to put our feet
in the dirty water before it disappeared
Children swam fully clothed
& we listened to the echo of mouths
through the canyon: *Don't leave*
You took a photograph
of the monsoon from a safe distance
When it finally caught up with us
you had to sprint the last mile back
to save the film

What an elegant sacrifice it is to be in love
To be in Real Love
& still, to have to exchange
money for food, two or three times a day
To have something to say
about the meager thoughts
that crop up in between

Weeds coming up through the concrete
that we are taught to eradicate
That would destroy us if we did

You wrote me a letter to say
you ate your lunch on the steps
of an office supply store
I read the letter while carrying
a twenty pound bag of ice
across a major highway intersection
All of the strings in me beginning to vibrate
toward a vestigial desire for weaponry

I am here with you
in a garden, or a wealthy front lawn
Here with my back in the scratching
grass & weeds, & your hand on my forehead
Here again—what is our purpose?

Art is hardly a purpose
unless you want to tell people
what to do & how to live

I live on the cliffs
of a permanent disbelief

in whatever it is we are feeding
I watch most people, down below
swiftly & tenderly replacing the lightbulbs
that backlight it at all hours

I do not blame you

I am thankful for all fathers
who never beckoned their children
into the woods, though I do wish I'd learned
how to use a chainsaw
Is this currency?

I know a few types of trees
& my body responds
to the sound of water approaching
Water is always approaching me
& in my dreams too
Not in waves or tsunamis
but in the signage that humans have made for it
Neat little brown / green rectangles
against the highway's field

You had a dream that haunts you
You were standing on a beach

watching the black, billowing smoke
approach from a distance
A psychic confirmed this
in 2010, so you regard my body
against the backdrop of apocalypse

We live in the city now
which means we can only access
the True World as escapists
If I open my mouth
about your forests, America
you mistake it for the knife
of my finger in your chest

or worse
You think that I am harmless

All art is meaningless
if it only serves to decorate
an intrinsically broken society

Gunshots Fired At Northeast Portland
Street Fair; Nine People Injured
Long, articulate arguments on the Internet
with people I'm not sure exist

The way the desire to witness violence
seeps into our lives without threat
& just lies there, pulsing
It's okay I remind us both
A sheet of paper on a gushing wound

Some days, I don't have anything
to sing about, & then I just want
other people to do it for me
I lay on the grass / a bed
& watch their enormous bodies soar upward
effortlessly, eternally
I watch the strings of continuous effort
disintegrate into the atmosphere
& I know money has nothing to do with it

Money has nothing to do with it
& yet it eases the suffering
We watch our friends drift
in & out of the money cloud
& then I want the strings to come back
as proof of how hard they tried
Culturally, this is very unpopular
Most people only really want to hear
thirteen-or-so highly polished studio tracks

They do not want the evidence
of struggle or fear just lying there
without the artist's commentary
that would justify their suspicions
that Being An Artist is truly very difficult

Why is it so difficult
you ask me, & I have no words for that either
You bring me my food & shelter
in your cupped hand

Music does not make
the sound of machines any easier to hear
when we wake up with our bodies entangled
& begin our series of thoughts

We have to keep each other calm
you tell me, & our limbs move soundlessly
toward a path that least resembles
what we are most terrified to define

I have no idea
if youth is really that great
though the world insists
on Youngness

I watch the news drift
in & out of our bedroom
attaching itself to familiar names

Gigantic, angular cities
vying to become one another
in the minds of those who walk through them

The Young do not like the world
to just sit there like a brown box
but that's what the world is
When they think about their own lifespan
they pull a flower from the soft dirt
as if it weighed a hundred pounds

A Great Writer tells me
When I wake up, I just get going
I have been attempting to arrange this lifestyle
for thirty years / I am lost

A city is a garden choked with great ideas
Deep in the guts of it there is a machinery
hinging on the principle
that its citizens will never understand it at all

There is a mystery enshrined
in the construction of power
Beautiful babies tumble out of it
& enter the workforce soundlessly
The soft fuzz of constant light rain

I am here with you, everyone talking
I get colder & smarter beneath all that sound
I get high & walk through my neighborhood
touching every plant on its bare shoulder
No one is trying to do me harm

I have paid & paid
to be held in the womb
of Invisible Freedom

I have something to chase / I have fifty more years

I discovered an extensive network
of thin trails leading from the center
of the field, just beginning there

Animals do not come around
just to remind us to leave

Two old women with long hair
place their hands on our stomachs
& begin a massive painting
of sweetgrass

I am standing on a dead tree
on mushrooms / you are in the forest
below me / we are in Arizona in the dark
& the moon is screaming at us
Go toward one another
She brings you to me in the dark
I am here

I am calm
I am here with you

now, sweeping the hair
with my hands, calm now
No one is trying to do you harm
The thing you think you are hearing
in the woods, your back turned to the mountain
Or in someone's voice shaking
pronouncing the name of what they want
is nameless, unless you name it
Unless you repeat the name in the dark

The thing I am seeking
that isn't a flag yet
The recording of it
rattling in my chest at night

When you seek love above all else
the world will reward you
with no money
When you learn how to stomach
atrocity, you will be asked to do it
again & again
It will be so difficult
& wonderful to start over
as you will be forced to do
many more times before your death

Whatever instrument you have chosen
to bear the weight of your whole self
Sit with it now
& let it be your life
Sit with your whole life now
& let it take its billowing shape before you
Get it over & done with

Sit down now
with the sound of your actual voice
& listen to what it begs you to do

Great floating beings above you
will ask you to keep them afloat
but you are not required to do this

Sleep
& drink clean water
Blackberries grow for free

I am here with you
Country, Love of My Life
I fight to find my body inside you
because I must, & you will thank me
You will make me beautiful
though you do not need me
I am going alone now
but alongside you
& I love you so entirely
I forget how to talk

LINER NOTES

Thank you to everyone here listening.

This book is for Jay Fiske: for your care, bravery, ∞, & true love. All of my flowers at your altar, forever. I love our life. Thank you for asking me to go swimming.

This book is for Jeff Schirmann: for your music, huge heart, & ways of being. You help me more than you will ever know. I'm so lucky I get to have you as a brother.

This book is for Emily May: for helping me see myself, my path, & the way the world works. I miss you and am grateful for you every day. Richard Manuel would be proud.

This book is for my parents, Bill & Denise: two mountains I learn from constantly. For my whole family, here & gone: I love you immensely & always.

This book owes itself to the following people, whose voices made it go: Alan Watts, Allen Ginsberg, Amy Lawless, Bill Callahan, Bob Dylan, Brandon Shimoda, Chan Marshall,

Dasha Shleyeva, David Foster Wallace, Dot Devota, Emily Kendal Frey, Frank Ocean, Gary Snyder, Graham Hunter Gregg, Hoa Nguyen, James Agee, Jenny Holzer, Joan Didion, Joanna Newsom, John Fahey, Jon-Michael Frank, Joni Mitchell, Kelly Knudtson, Mathias Svalina, Neil Young, Nick Younes, Nico, Nina Simone, Patti Smith, Paul Thomas Anderson, Phil Elverum, Ravi Shankar, Richard Brautigan, Robin Pecknold, Stevie Nicks, Townes Van Zandt, Tyler Brewington, Van Morrison, & Zachary Schomburg. Thank you all.

These poems have appeared in various forms in the following places: *Everyday Genius*, *Forklift/Ohio*, The Greying Ghost Pamphlet Series, *Hobart*, *Monster House Press*, PENAmerica, *Poor Claudia*, *Sixth Finch*, & the *Sonora Review*. Thank you to the editors of these journals for publishing my work.

Thanks finally & especially to Janaka Stucky and everyone at Black Ocean for their care and support in bringing this book into the world.